THOUGHTS of a Ten-Year-Old

Master Sanith Santhasa Piyadigamage

AuthorHouse™ UK
1663 Liberty Drive
Bloomington, IN 47403   USA
www.authorhouse.co.uk
Phone: 0800.197.4150

Published by AuthorHouse 11/07/2018

ISBN: 978-1-7283-8029-2 (sc)
ISBN: 978-1-7283-8030-8 (e)

Print information available on the last page.

This book is printed on acid-free paper.

authorHOUSE®

Contents

Foreword

When I was asked to write a foreword for this book entitled *Thoughts of a Ten Year Old*, by Sanith, I expected it to be in the form of a diary with simple anecdotes. But what has been written in this book by this very young author is fascinating. He has presented almost all aspects of thoughts of a 10 year old encapsulating diverse themes while showing a philosophical edge to his thinking. Most importantly, his writing is very coherent. The maturity he shows in this field he probably acquired by submitting articles to papers and magazines beginning when he was only 4 to 5 years old and the first book he wrote some years back. He has used words to bridge the gaps between emotions and thoughts, showing a maturity far exceeding his age.

Indral K. Perera, Emeritus Professor

Preface

Wonder in mysteries of nature
With the passion and desire to venture,
Choosing books, drones, and animals,
Choosing right, leaving out wrong.
A small figure is still in the making
To a human worth knowing . . .

I drown myself in books, having no regard for time. Documentaries on World War II, Area 51, and space expeditions could easily turn me into a couch potato, but I avoid munching when seated. Animals are the ones I love to mingle freely with.

Having reached serene Dubai when I was just over a year, I kept on jotting down my thoughts on regular intervals.

Be a voice not an echo.

—Albert Einstein

It was my teacher I presented my first book to when just 5 years old. The book of six small pages of handwritten words she embraced with utmost kindness. It was the newspapers and magazines, I went onto outline my thoughts to, as next.

Not every rider is a horseman and not every horseman is a knight.
—His Highness Sheikh Mohammed bin Rashid Al Maktoum

Achieving greater heights makes us unique. The right guidance and persistence enable us to reach goals. I began to jot down, focusing on my goal.

Today, I take great pleasure in presenting you with *Thoughts of a Ten Year Old.*

Writing

The moments and people I have come across in this world of limitless possibilities are vast. I love meeting people who are gracious. I love to dwell in moments I can treasure. But the choice has not been mine most of the time. A chain of a different metal altogether it's been like.

The goal is the hope in which we strive, and experience is the school in which we learn. This is my way of feeling.

What about you?

Experience I define as knowledge. So tell me: what's your method of keeping track of your knowledge?

I have a habit of taking notes of my thoughts, observations, and happenings. I love to write.

I discovered the beauty of blending my thoughts into words.

I know well words strengthen our memories and enable sharing.

Getting a hold of my old notebook with red horizontal lines, I reckon, was one of the best moments. The small book was filled with various thoughts of mine. I had written them when I was just six. Has it ever occurred to you to find your own self back on a timeline? It was one of my rare experiences.

I saw my handwriting, words, and thoughts. The writer seemed different in thinking in comparison to the present days.

It's amazing how fast someone can become a stranger.

—KushandWizdom

Has the passage of time changed me or my priorities?
Discovering my own self back in time was truly amazing.
The beauty of writing!

Reading

Reading and writing are more like a thread and a needle to me. It's the correlation of the two that bring in the best. The books—my gateway to the past, the present, and the future—are the main source to my tunnel of knowledge.

Trenton Lee Stewart's *The Extraordinary Education of Nicholas Benedict,* Roald Dahl's *Esio Trot,* and Michael Morpurgo's *Shadow* are some of the all-time favourites. I still could lose myself in them.

Protecting the lives of animals was of utmost importance to Nazis, who tortured and killed millions of Jews. Vegetarians in ancient Greece offered vegetables as sacrifices to their gods. If not for books, I would not have known any of the above. If not for books, most of the historical facts of humankind would not have survived.

> There are two possibilities, either we are alone in the universe or we are not. Both are equally terrifying.
>
> —Sir Arthur C. Clarke

The prediction of the great science writer and futurist initiated in-depth space explorations.

Then again, I sense another case of two possibilities that could equally be terrifying: either being clueless of the importance of reading or the nonexistence of books on the Planet Earth.[1]

Could it be a reality one day? I hope not.

"Reading maketh a person worth living and knowing," and that's how I feel about reading.[2]

---

[1] *Quotes by the Author
[2] *Quotes by the Author

Reflection

Each person does his or her own reflection in different ways, from a businessman thinking about his new marketing strategies to a gamer who feels flattered about his moves. Some share, and some brood. I love the combination the most.

We learn from mistakes we feel like speaking of. But some can be too embarrassing to share. Try converting the experience into learning.

I like that habit.

Being the only child, I partner up with my parents in reflection. I love to hear of their past before I go to sleep. I listen to their thoughts of people and happenings. I compare mine with them.

I feel important when they appreciate my views.

Reflection can guide us within priorities.

We must get the best of the experience wisely. Then nothing will be a waste eventually.

Oranges in My Land

Ayesha struggled to save her grandmother. She lived with no assurance of seeing the dawn or the dusk of each day. The debris and the poverty-stricken lives showed no signs of ending further losses or misery.

The checkpoints, sandbags, and enemy flags: Elizabeth Laird's *Oranges in No Man's Land* was one of the lessons I spent much time to comprehend.

My school, classrooms, teachers, and friends—my life—are different from Ayesha's. There are no sandbags or enemy flags I should take note of. The path is cordial, halcyon, and encouraging.

The school is "a place we walk in strong and walk out stronger."[3] It's not just the projects or the worksheets that nourish our thinking.

I like what we discuss during moral education lessons. As a boy living in the world's most cosmopolitan city, it's vital knowing the values of empathy and compassion.

---

[3] *Quotes by the Author

Friends

Helen Keller said, "I would rather walk with a friend in the dark, than alone in the light." Would you?

The friends and friendship. The ones who are willing to share.

Mine differ from one to another. I feel it's not easy choosing good friends. The process is delicate and testing. The right ones will help us find hope and courage when we need them the most.

Let time decide who you could really count on. Never rush your decisions or judgements. Impressions can be baseless without careful observations. I have learned bitter lessons in rushing to conclusions. Maybe you are like me.

It's from a book that I understood the importance of surrounding yourself with those of the same goals.

Judging who we really are will not be hard, looking at whom we sit with!

Holidays

Summer holiday leaves me with no boundaries to brood. Naval ships, air crash investigations, and space fascinate me in every way possible. The unexpected mysteries and alluring wonders—how could someone not be fascinated by them?

"Where there is preparation, there is no fear" are Hwan Kee's words of wisdom.

The oldest Chinese art of self-defence, kung fu, fascinates me in every way. For many, training is about being better than someone else.

Kung fu placed a different vision in front of me. It taught me *the importance of being better than yesterday.* The simple vision brings me confidence and inspiration.

The traditional teachings will help you understand the right outcome. They help build character. The discipline, patience, and perseverance you gain from the teachings are immense.

Discover the wonders and your possibilities.

Courage

"Learn from the bad and stick with the good" is one of my favourite slogans.

Good times and bad times, most definitely, part and partial.

The situations have differed just as my friends. Truthfulness and appreciation I saw sticking together. Yes, it did most of the time. But losing what I love for being true is no secret too. Moments are enough. That I can recall.

Then what? I wondered at times.

Courage is a big word in the bigger world.

What's courage? Why should one have it, and when? Is it to back your friend who was unrefined or to aid a stranger who was agitated by your friend?

What would you have done?

Standing up for right, even in the presence of fear, is courage in the eyes of the great men and women of the past.

The courage you knew I hope was no different.

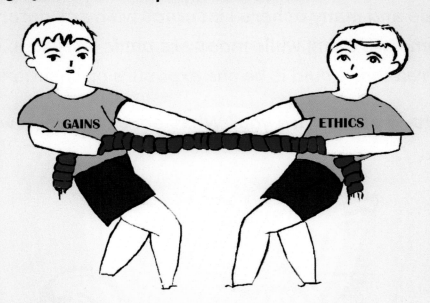

Tell me: would there be a better time to remind the world of the meaning of courage?

People and Situations

The friends and many others I interact with act differently to one another. Some are calm, while most are panic-stricken. What do you think is the reason? Could it be the exposure or their nature?

What sort of person are you? What sort of person would you like to be?

The story of twelve young Thai soccer players and their coach showed the world the power of mindfulness and the benefits of staying calm.

Letting go or relaxing is never quitting.

Life is not about achievements others set for us. Life is not about others' opinions.

It's ours to live—to live right and well.

Many I come across lose their temper in a blink of an eye and then realise the payback is heavy. The wise people point out that frustration and anger are entirely our own creations.

Perhaps a little change of outset, instead of keeping constant contact with screens. Have you ever tried?

Having a bit more enthusiasm for nature, books, or any other living creatures could help regulate our emotions. They say it reduces the "stress" everyone's talking of.

Good or bad is created by our way of thinking.

"Self control is strength"

Be what you expect from yourself, not just what others want you to be.

Growing Up

Time sails fast, and we navigate our own ships. There is so much we do from the time we open our eyes until we call it a day.

Lessons learned from failure, happiness shared of glory, and daunting efforts to become what you want, I reckon, are fulfilling moments of growing.

Think a little deeply. Where do you fit in?

What we do daily takes place within and without. Thoughts, words, and deeds become driven by our way of life.

We no longer step into primary school and then head towards secondary school. The teachers and the settings differ. The words are big, and expectations are bigger. Our best friend is no longer a candy dweller and is more into philately.

I guess you are yet to figure out who you want to be when you grow up.

We are growing and will continue to grow.

The Final Chapter

The final chapter is yours to complete.

_____

_____

_____

_____

_____

_____

_____

_____

_____

_____

_____

_____

_____

_____

_____

_____

_____

_____

_____

_____

_____

_____

_____

Printed in the United States
By Bookmasters